Modern day words and wisdom
for young women starting their journey in life.

Have You
Filled Her Backpack?

Elizabeth Kokalis

Backpack Publishing LLC
Oak Creek, Wisconsin
backpackpublishing@gmail.com

Dream...Write...Inspire...Do it!

You may find that this book is not only for young women and parents to read, but for anyone who wants to fill their own backpack.

Dedication

To my daughter Amalia, who has embarked on her life's journey

and

To my son for keeping this book a secret until now.

The Road Trip

(Contents)

Acknowledgements

Dan, thank you for encouraging me to write this book and for your suggestions; they were priceless.

Elias, I appreciate you reviewing this book; it was very helpful.

Cliff, I am grateful for your artistic ideas.

Diane, thank you for some of the editing tips of the first draft over a cup of coffee.

Christos, thank you for your on-going enthusiasm to have me publish this book.

Amalia, thank you for putting up with me all these months before you head out on your journey. Your editing perspective was precious.

A final thank you to: my Mother, my Father, my Brother and my longtime family friend Linda, who did their best in filling my backpack.

Preface

My daughter's 18th Birthday was soon approaching along with her high school graduation. I didn't know what to buy her. I wanted to give her something special; a gift that she would always remember.

We had been squabbling on and off for several months. It was the typical teenage girl and mother fights. What I really wanted to do during these times was give her, well, "a piece of my mind" so to speak. That is when giving her some heartfelt words of wisdom, and advice came to light.

My gift to her is a collection of what I have learned or should have learned throughout my life so far. This guide includes some day to day things that I might have forgotten to share with her. I feel that the girls we love and care about should have enough information and guidance to make good choices when they go off on their own journey.

Since giving her this book, we have become closer and our relationship has surprisingly strengthened. She has even provided me with some of her own words of wisdom and advice which are included in this book. Imagine that: she read the words and had her own reflections.

Introduction

All of us have unique family dynamics: single, divorced, married or blended, but one thing we all have in common is that we want the best for our young girls starting their journeys.

Clearly, the world today is fast paced and we need to keep up with the changing times and the technology; be careful not to lose signal. There are also some old values and words of wisdom that shouldn't be forgotten. Sometimes we need to get back to the basics. The past generations of parents often didn't talk about what young people are facing or will in the future; therefore some of us were left to wing it. Why not give the new generation information to prepare them for the future?

I wrote this book to be used as reference to inspire people to have conversations. The method used throughout the book provides the reader important messages: snippets of modern day information and also some wise sayings or proverbs that hold true today. Inside you will also find quotes, one-liners, and advice in a contemporary fashion. The chapters are written mostly from personal reflections, experiences and observations. You'll read about job interviewing tips to practical relationship advice. The first chapter starts with daily rituals and the last ends with a catch- all collection, which I couldn't easily fit elsewhere. You can choose to skip around from chapter to chapter or read it straight through cover to cover.

Now, let's start filling that backpack!

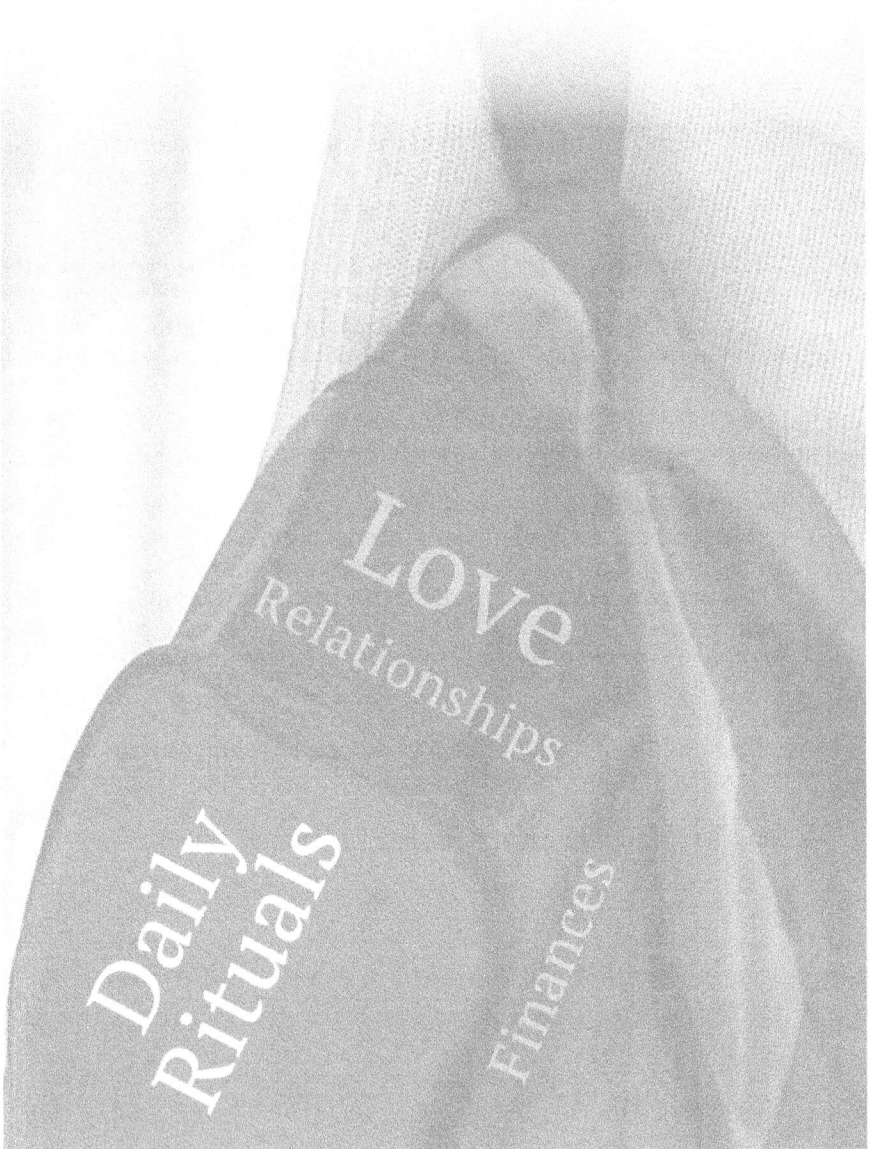

CHAPTER 1

Love

Relationships

Daily
Rituals

Finances

It's a beautiful new day every morning, wake up with a smile.

Wish people a "good morning". It's a wonderful way to start your day and theirs too.

Remember to brush and floss your teeth.

Take a few minutes to make your bed. It's your first accomplishment of the day. It can set the tone of your day in a positive way.

Stay healthy: wash your hands often.

Remember not to salt your food before you taste it.

Try not to create or be involved in drama, instead leave it for the girls who have nothing better to do.

See problems as opportunities for growth.

Have a good pair of shoes to walk and work in.

When you don't want to cry, squeeze your butt cheeks...it works!

Write timely thank you notes.

When you are going for a run or walking in the street, always face towards the direction of oncoming traffic. It sounds strange, but you can see the cars coming.

Trust your intuition or "gut" feelings.

Read, Read, Read
Feed, Feed, Feed
Your mind....

Learn about politics, world and current affairs.

Laugh whenever you can: it feels great.

Remember that nothing good happens after midnight.

Pick out your clothes the night before; it saves time in the morning.

Make good decisions and choices.

Remember to wear sunscreen, sunburn hurts and too much sun causes wrinkles later in life.

The elders have wisdom; listen to them.

"Pan Metron Ariston"
Translation: Everything in moderation.
(An unknown ancient Greek philosopher)

Listen to and appreciate a variety of music.

Think before you speak and know when to keep your mouth closed.

Speak your mind, but do it respectfully and with grace.

Be honest but never hurtful.
Always think of how it would make you feel to hear
something unpleasant about yourself.

If you don't ask the question; you'll never know the answer.

Happiness is a choice; it's a setting in your mind that you can adjust.

Remember to dance.

It frees your soul and

illuminates your spirit.

Dance whenever

you have the chance.

Celebrate the little things in life: completing a tough project, waking up to the spring aroma of lilacs, wearing your favorite jacket and finding money in the pockets, or receiving unexpected hugs and kisses from a loved one.

Be positive, stay positive and you will attract the positive in your life. No one likes to be around negativity; it only breeds more negative feelings in people. Therefore, surround yourself with positive people.

Practice random acts of kindness;
it's a blast to do and people won't expect it.

Timing is everything and having patience is important.
You might not get the results you want if you don't time your actions.

You are sometimes judged by the company you keep.
Have you heard of guilt by association?

Try not to waste time and energy on things that may not happen.

If you want to walk and listen to your iPod, use only one ear bud.
You can't hear what is happening around you, or if someone comes
up behind if you have both buds in.

Wear cute sun glasses.

Have clean, nice looking fingernails and treat yourself to a pedicure.

Be kind, gentle and loving.

Don't swear or use the f- bomb; it can be offensive to others.
There are more intelligent words to use to get your point across.

Remember to always take off your make-up before bedtime.

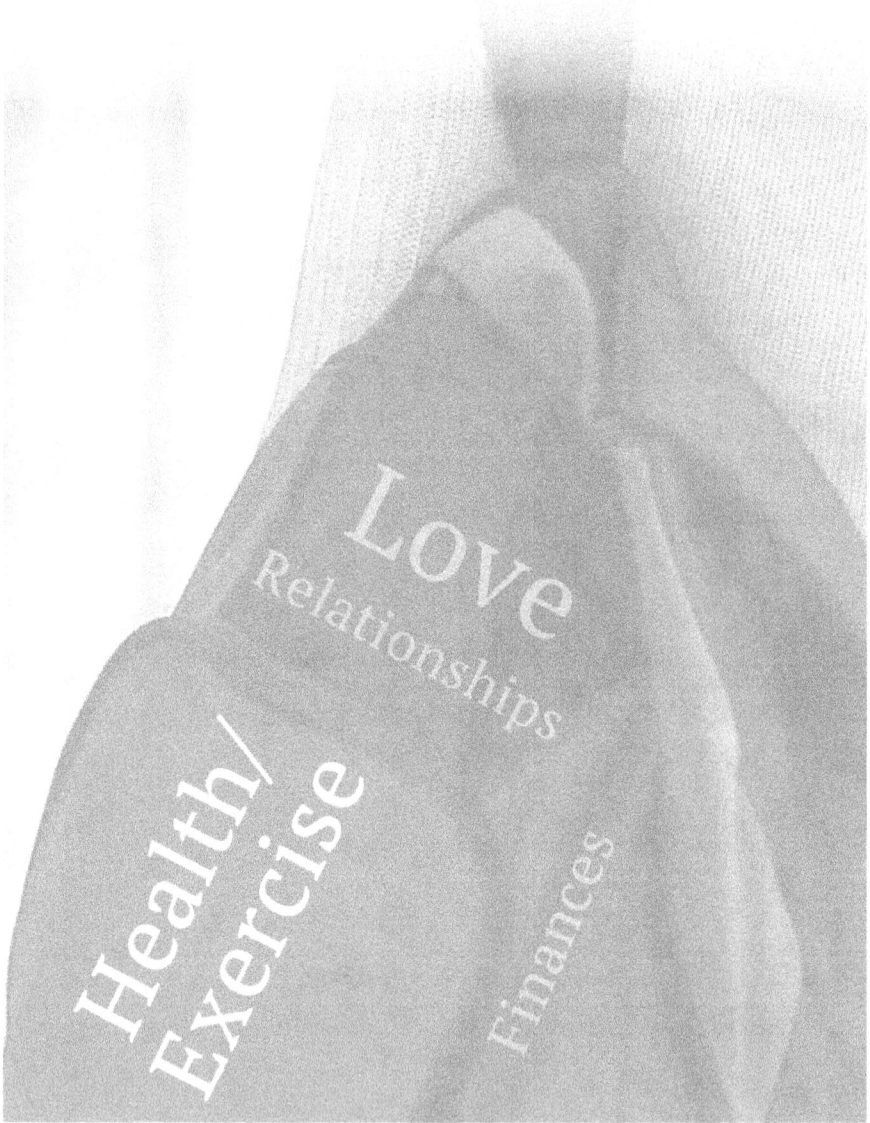

CHAPTER 2

Love

Relationships

Health/ Exercise

Finances

Alcohol may be a solution in chemistry,
but it's only a temporary one in life.

Remember don't leave your drink unattended;
someone may slip a "mickey" in it.

Try yoga once... then go back and try it again.

Learn to enjoy green tea because it's good for your health.

Don't smoke; it quickly becomes an expensive habit and it's very difficult to quit.

Don't do drugs. They are illegal and you could go to jail.
This would change your life forever.
Note: "Not inhaling" is still participating.

When you turn 21 have a drink but drink responsibly.

Heavy drinking can age your face.
It speeds up the aging process on your skin, causing early wrinkles.
The consumption of large quantities of alcohol dehydrates your body;
and the hydration is required for youthful skin.

Be focused and disciplined.

Find an exercise class you like.

Do some stretching daily to be fit.

Overeating is not healthy and neither is under eating. If you are concerned about your eating habits don't wait too long to talk to someone about it.

Try every day to drink half of your body weight in water by converting your weight into ounces from pounds. For example, if you weigh 130 pounds, you would drink 65 ounces of water daily. Drinking a lot of water can helps control calories and replaces fluids lost during exercise.

Have breakfast; it helps kick start your brain function.

Eating protein rich foods daily is important for your diet. Protein helps your body repair cells among other things.
Protein rich foods are: nuts, eggs, chicken, beef, pork or fish.

Eat fruits and vegetables every day. There are many to choose from. Find some you like. Healthy habits start when you're young.

Try to make fish part of your weekly diet. It's packed with protein and nutrients. If you don't like the taste of fish, dip it in ketchup. Almost everything tastes better with ketchup.

If you have a doctor's appointment, write a list of questions in advance that you would like to ask.

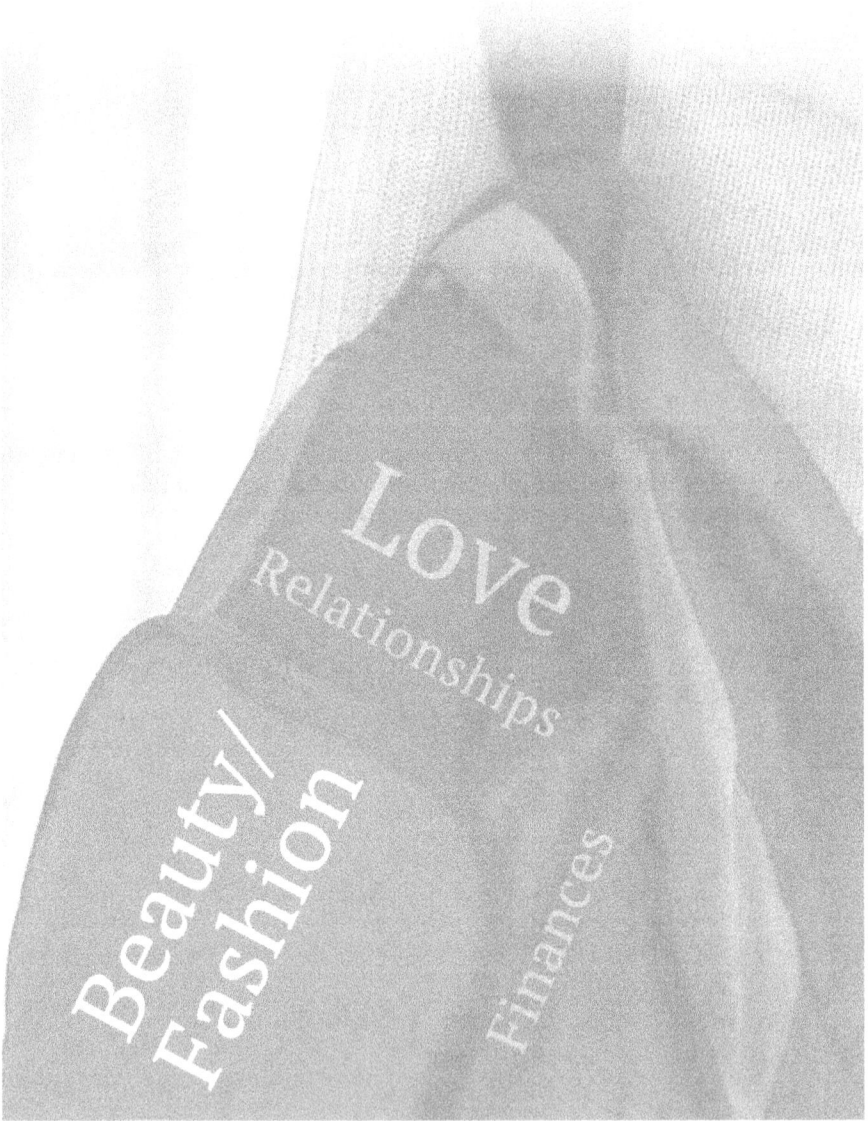

CHAPTER 3

Love

Relationships

Beauty/
Fashion

Finances

Be a woman who has a good heart, fabulous smile, and a stimulating mind.
Your body and clothes are only window dressing of the beauty in you.

Beauty starts from the inside and works itself out.

A beautiful woman pleases the eye for a moment.
If her heart is beautiful, it will last a lifetime.

If you feel good about yourself you will look good too.

Sometimes what you wear determines your mood and how you feel.

Classic fashion is timeless. Here is a list of items that are must have in your wardrobe:

- A white blouse
- A black skirt
- One pair of black pants
- One pair of "power pumps"
- One "little black dress" known as the (LBD)

Note: A little black dress is a fashion iconic staple. Women have been wearing a version of the LBD for almost a century. It can be worn to a wedding by accessorizing it with pretty jewelry or a scarf. You can also wear it to a funeral by dressing it down wearing little or no jewelry. If you're attending an important meeting you can throw on a colorful blazer or sweater and cute shoes and you are all set to make an impression. Also, if you add a strand of pearls to your LBD, it will give a certain *je ne sais quoi* (a pleasant quality that is hard to describe) that will charm everyone. (They don't have to be expensive pearls). The LBD can be worn for almost any occasion. It will last for several years and through many fashion seasons.

Red lipstick is classic and powerful.
If worn for the right occasion, it will be a "wow" factor that will
captivate everyone.
Try to find the right shade for your skin tone.

The color black is easy to work with on a limited budget. It's easy to mix
and match with other colorful pieces. The use of accessories like belts,
scarves and jewelry can enhance or change up the look. Try using a splash
of color; it's amazing.

Color-code your closet to find items easier. You can organize your closet by
dark colors to light colors with all other colors in between.
Try using plastic hangers and face all clothes the same direction.

If you buy a new shirt, pair of pants or pair of shoes,
let another item go from your closet.
Practice the one- in- one- out rule.
(This rule is a way to have control of things you own and to avoid clutter)

Donate your old clothes. It can make a difference in someone's life. Consider donating to a shelter or other charitable organizations.

All girls have different body styles so you need to wear things that flatters your unique figure.

Embrace your body whether you are full figured, curvy, thin, short or tall. Rock your body with pretty clothes.

Your clothing makes and sends a statement about who you are. What is the message and statement you want to send?

Accentuate the body part that is your best feature.

A nude or beige colored shoe will make your legs look longer.

A gathered waistline, if you are full figured and curvy, tends to give an appearance of looking shorter.

Wear stripes vertically with a smaller stripe pattern.

Wear smaller prints rather than larger ones.

Own a clothing iron and ironing board.

Use nail polish to stop a run in your panty hose or tights.

Try not to have your panty lines show. That goes for your thong too.
Wear nude color panties with no lines.

.

When you wear a swim suit, take care of your bikini line.

Make sure your bra fits you properly and
try not to show too much cleavage.

Your bras eventually will stretch and lose elasticity and support;
replace your bras often, especially the most favorite ones.

Don't pop your zits. Your fingers, no matter how clean, have bacteria on
them and make it worse.

Don't EVER use a razor to shape your eyebrows!
Instead, pluck or wax them.
Also, don't make them too thin.

Try not to wash your hair every day.
Shampooing your hair makes it oilier because it traps the oils, making your hair dry out and causing breakage. Change up your hairstyle and put it in a pony-tail on the days you don't wash it or use dry shampoo.

When you comb or brush your hair start from the bottom and work your way up it helps detangle and prevents hair from splitting and breaking.

Only use a brush on your hair when it's dry not wet to prevent breakage.

Beauty fades but the heart remains.

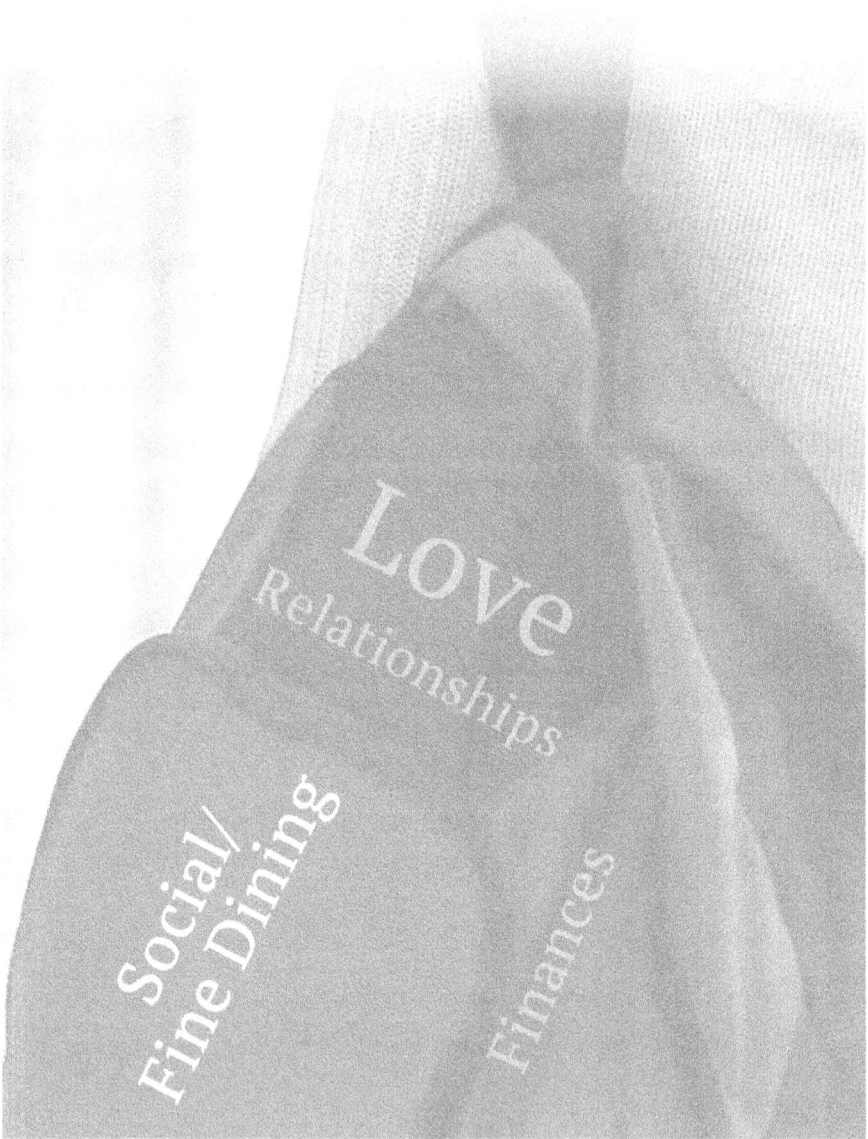

CHAPTER 4

Love

Relationships

Social/
Fine Dining

Finances

Dining etiquette varies by country and culture.
(When in Rome be a Roman).

If you're attending a formal dinner that has multiple eating utensils, start using the utensils placed the farthest on either side of the plate.

The spoon and fork above your plate are usually used for dessert. Good rule of thumb, use whichever makes the most sense; the fork for cake and spoon for ice-cream.

When eating with one or more people, wait until everyone has been served before you start eating.

What to do with the napkin? Well, place it on your lap. Don't stuff it on the top of your shirt. When you're finished with your meal, nicely fold it and place it to the left of your plate.

It's not polite to reach across the table or over a person for anything. Ask for it to be passed to you. Food should be passed counter clockwise or to your right in American style of dining.

"Excuse me; can you please pass me the salt?"
The salt and pepper should be passed
"as a pair."

If you don't wish to have what's in the bowl being passed to you, say thank you and keep passing the bowl; don't put it down.
Keep the train moving.

If you are served soup, scoop with the spoon away from you. Never pick up the cup or bowl and slurp the remaining soup unless the culture dictates it. In Japan, slurping the remaining soup is a sign it was delicious. However, this is not acceptable in other Asian cultures, and especially not in the USA.

Don't cut all your meat up at once. Cut only 1-2 bite sized pieces at a time. Place your knife down and continue using the hand you normally eat with. Repeat until you are finished eating. This is the American style of dining. It is also referred to as the cut and switch style.

European countries use the Continental style of dining. It seems more practical. They hold the fork in one hand and keep the knife in the other hand never switching the utensils back and forth. They cut and eat, cut and eat.

Are you wondering what to do with the bread?
Surprisingly, you break it up into pieces. Place a small amount of butter on your plate and butter only what you are ready to eat.

Remember elbows off the table.
However, if you travel to Russia, rest your wrists on the dinner table so they are visible.

What's sorbet?
It's like a fruity frozen slushy with a little thicker consistency;
everyone's dream!
It's actually served to cleanse and refresh your palate for the next course.

When you're dining in a restaurant, if the silverware falls off the table
don't look for it or pick it up. You can pretend like it never happened and
ask the server for a new one.

In some countries like China, Turkey and parts of the Middle East, a big
belch after a good meal indicates it was delicious and is a compliment to
the chef.

It's fun to learn some toasts in other languages. Some of the same toasts
are used by several countries. Here is a list of a few of them: Prost
(German), Nazdravie (Polish), Ziveli (Serbian), Lech aim (Hebrew),
Gan bai (Chinese), Ya mas (Greek), Salud (Spanish), Cin-Cin (Italian), and
Viva (Brazilian).

If you are invited to dinner at someone's house, always bring a small gift like flowers, dessert, or something homemade.
When you turn 21 years old a bottle of wine is also appropriate.
It's the gesture that counts.
Note: Don't buy the cheap stuff; you may have to drink it too!

If you have dinner at someone's home offer to help clear the table, but wait until everyone is finished with their meal.

Throughout the world, the one commonality we all share is that a meal brings us together.

bon appetite, buon appetito, guten appetit, buen provecho, *kali orexi,* or enjoy your meal!

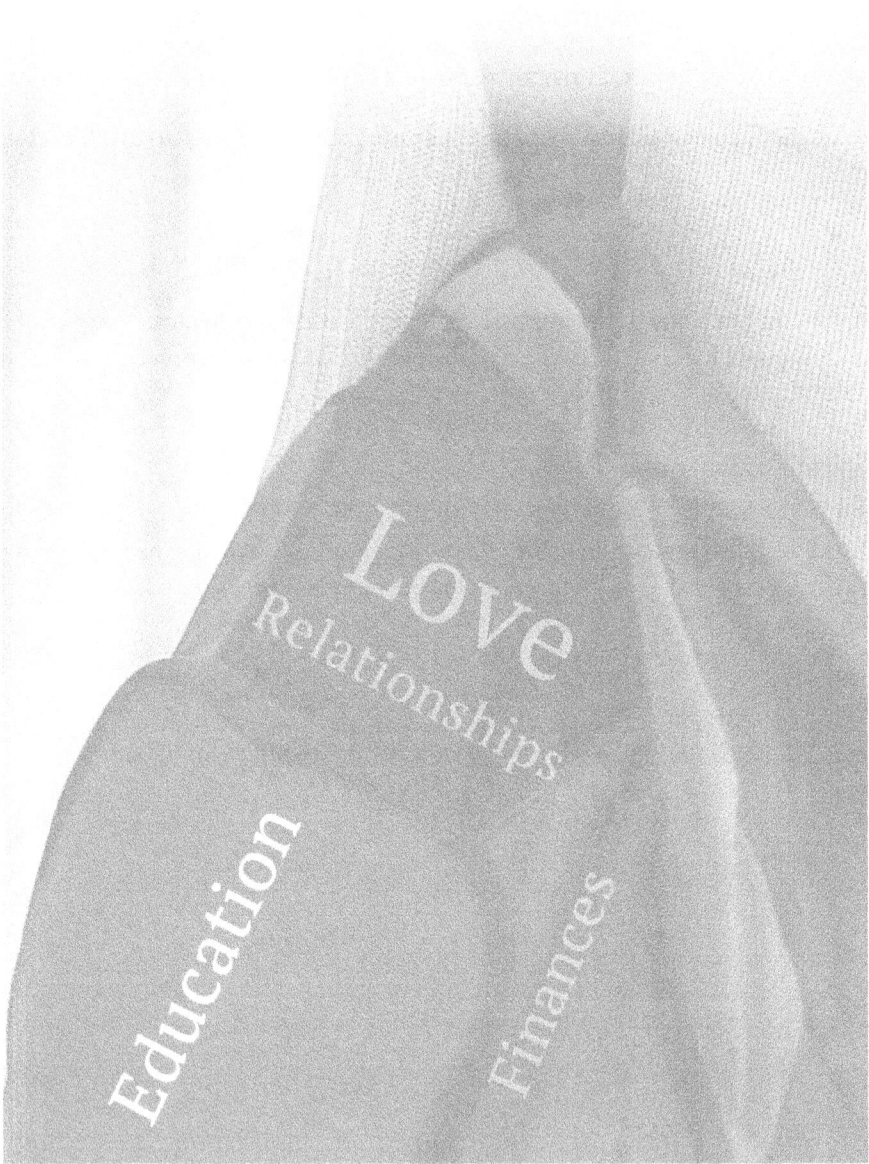

CHAPTER 5

Love
Relationships
Education
Finances

Get an education! It's something that no one can ever take away from you.

Community colleges offer many career studies. It's a less expensive alternative if you are unsure of your career path.

Your first semester of college will be challenging. It's a new school, new environment, possible new roommates and teachers that have higher expectations. You'll be okay.

When in class or at a seminar, always try to sit in front.
You are there to learn.

Professors while teaching like to also provide their personal opinions or points of view; take in the information, but create your own opinions.

Avoid the fearful "freshman 15" by exercising and eating healthy meals and snacks.

College is the some of the best years of your life; find your balance. When you're in college, you have to manage your time between classes, studying, work, friends and activities. Earning good grades is very important. College life is a juggling act requiring balance.

College can be stressful. Make sure you have a network of people you can to talk if you need encouragement.

Know that a student charged with a drug related offense could lose the financial aid they received.

School comes first before going out with your friends. Be focused and stay on course.

Strive to be able to support yourself.

Be a perpetual student of knowledge.

"Strong minds discuss ideas,
Average minds discuss events,
Weak minds discuss people."
~Socrates

Try to be well-rounded in your conversations.

Be the best at everything you do; it will make you feel good
at the end of the day.

Make new friends that you share common interests with and maybe even
consider starting a study group.

Join a club.

Having a variety of knowledge is power and strength.
Note: It's also helpful when you're playing board games.

Study..... Study..... Study!

Sleep is very important: you need to rest your body and mind.

When learning and memorizing new material find techniques that help you recall and retain information: using acronyms, word associations, creating a song/story, or making flash cards.

Reviewing material before bedtime is a secret way to retain information.

Cramming for a test may be good for the short run; it's not good for long term retention of information. Reviewing material daily is best.

You should try to unplug yourself from the stimulation your electronics provide for at least one hour a day. This means take a break from your cell phone and social media. Your phone and computer like your brain needs to recharge; otherwise you can't use it effectively.

"Whatever is good to know is difficult to learn."
~Greek Proverb
(Don't give up.)

Be curious and ask questions.

Apply for scholarships: it could be a way to lower your tuition.

Be aware of deadlines and be sure you don't miss them.

"Successful people are not afraid to think."
~Daniel V. Gonzalez

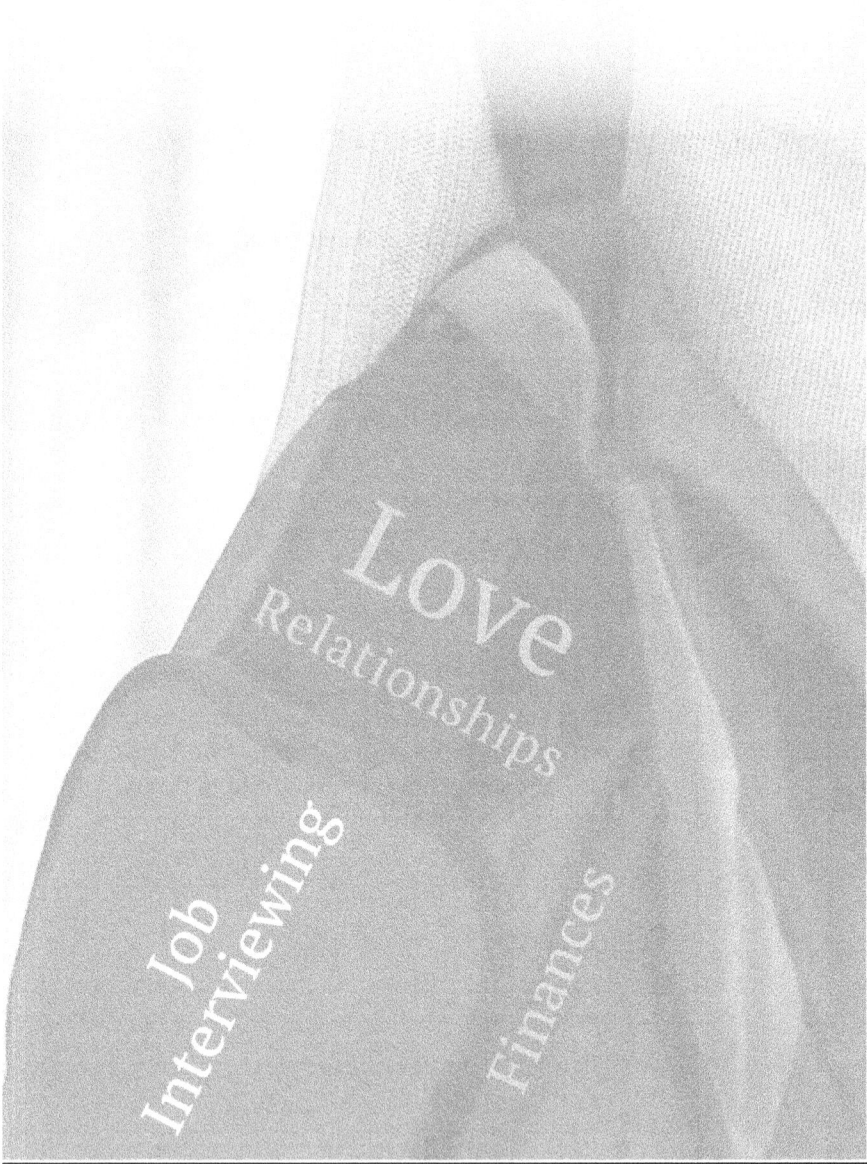

CHAPTER 6

Love

Relationships

Job Interviewing

Finances

Finding a job is a job in itself.

Have confidence in yourself.

Subscribe to LinkedIn and start networking.
You could be exposed to people who may have a connection you need.

When using someone as a reference, always ask the person for their permission first. Remember to consider past teachers and coaches as possible referees.

Prepare an elevator speech on who you are.
An elevator speech is a 30 second summary of who you are and what you like to do. The speech is called this way in reference to the time span of riding in an elevator and, of course, always facing forward.

Think about how you would be an asset
to the company you are applying to.

Be prepared. Do some research on the company you are interviewing with
and maybe even mention a well-known fact. Also, they might ask you
questions to see what you know about the company.

Employers like a team player, and a person who is honest and ethical.

Think of stories ahead of time that you could cite to support your answer
to interviewing questions.

During your interview don't use slang or texting language like LOL.

Don't forget to bring several copies of your resume along and have it readily available.

Have a few questions for you to ask the interviewer.

Read and remember the company's "mission statement".

Dress nicely and appropriately.

Be on time or even a few minutes early for your interview.

Have a firm handshake in your interview, but a ladies hand shake when it's appropriate.

Don't chew gum.

Remember not to fold your arms.

Stand up straight and don't slouch.

Remember to smile!

Know it's not inappropriate to ask what the starting wage is.

Explain how you have what it takes to do the job.
Sell yourself; it's your time to shine!

Thank your interviewer for their time.

Don't post on social media about your interview.

Send the interviewer a thank you via email.
It may seem outdated, but also send your interviewer
a hand written thank you note.

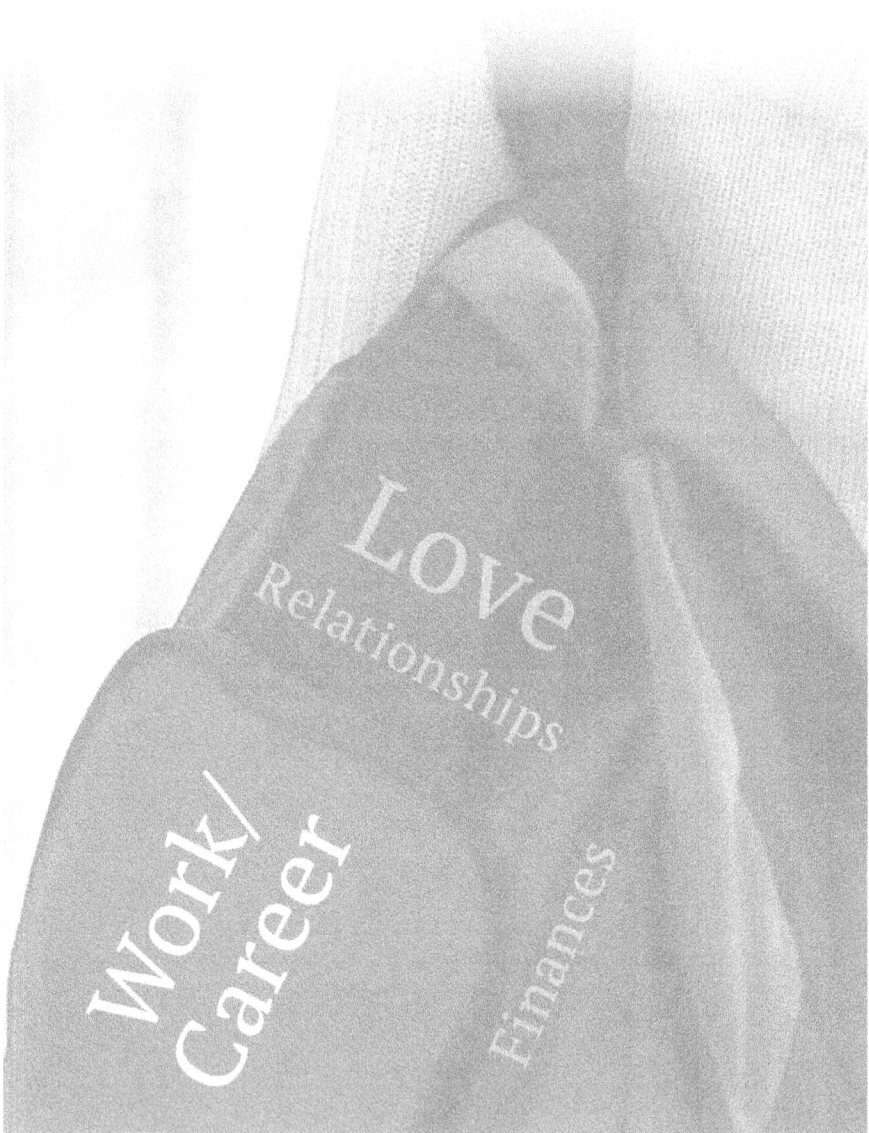

CHAPTER 7

Love
Relationships
Work/
Career
Finances

It's important to be a woman first. Be true to yourself.
This is the foundations that will springboard you to other roles in your life."
~Kathy Hust

Have a professional photo taken every few years to keep up with
your new look and maturity. You never know when you will need it.

Become familiar with the 80/20 Rule or the Pareto Principal.
This concept can also be applied to your job or career;
20% of the people do 80% of the work.
Be the 20%!

Dress for the job you want, not the one you have.

Never take credit for someone else's work.

If you choose to be a career woman, have a work/ life balance.
The creating of balance requires time management skills.
Don't be too proud to ask for help if you need it.

If you chose to be married while maintaining your job or career,
discuss the sharing of responsibilities with your spouse. If your choice
is to be a stay-home mom, try to work at least part time to keep your
skills and mind sharp.
Note: This is assuming you're not married to a Neurosurgeon making
$900K a year.

Try not to participate in office gossip.
"He said...She said..."
Blah-Blah-Blah
Yada, Yada, Yada
It's a time waster.

Never compromise your integrity.
"Integrity is doing the right thing when no one is watching."
~ C.S. Lewis

Keep an on-going list of your achievements or successes when time comes for your review and a raise in pay. That way, you will have feedback and documentation for your boss or supervisor. This can be a letter of praise someone sent you about the good job you've done, a thank you email someone sent, a positive survey comment or a suggestion that you have made which was incorporated.

Know your loyalties and keep them.

Have big goals and break them down into smaller goals so you can achieve them and not feel frustrated about how long it could potentially take to reach the big goal. This can be for work or your personal life.
Reward yourself along the way.

Write your goals down. If you don't, they don't count.

Don't accept being average.

Be a leader, not a follower.
If everyone was a leader would there be followers?
Yes, because some people can only follow.

Prepare the night before for the work you do the following day.

Try to make a difference.

Be clever and creative.

It's easier to find a new job if you already have one.

If you ever want to complain, you chose the job or career you have.
Try not to be afraid to change it if you can.
~Amalia Melissourgos

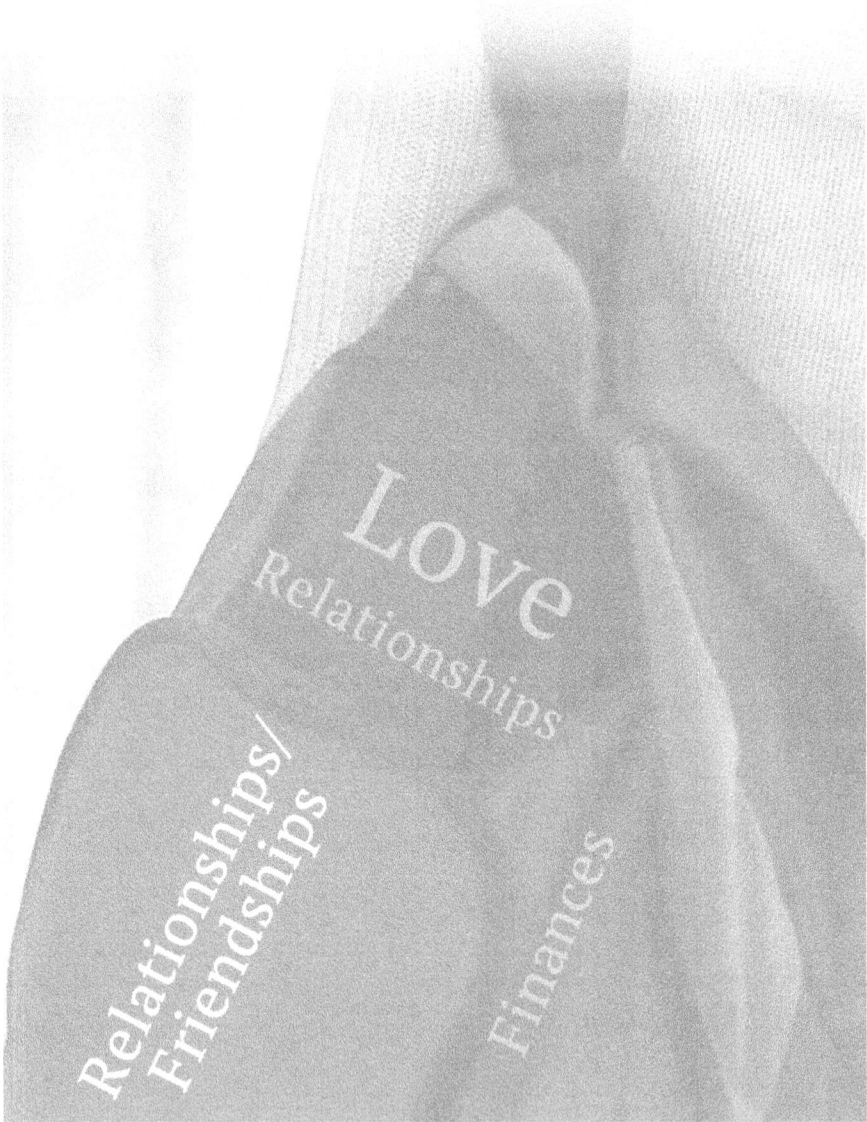

CHAPTER 8

Love
Relationships

Relationships/
Friendships

Finances

Seek out the good in people.

Remember: make the bed when you are an overnight guest in someone's home.

Try to see things from other people's points of view; especially in politics or religion.

Don't burn any bridges. You might have to cross the same river some day in the future. It's easier for you to cross that bridge if it's still standing.

Pay attention not to play the blame game seek understanding instead.

Guys will look at other women. It's true and in their DNA. However, a GENTLEMAN never gets caught looking and would never do it in front of you.

If a guy ever tells you he doesn't want to be in a relationship, BELIEVE him. This is one thing that guys are completely honest about. So, don't give up your single status just yet, until you are boyfriend and girlfriend.

If you have already made your guy a priority, make sure you're not just an option for him. If you are an option, you need to re-set YOUR priorities.

No guy is worth crying over.
If he is a WORTHY guy, he will never want to see or make you cry.

"Don't just look at the flower. Look at the seed."
~Elias Kokalis

Most people like to be admired so let them know you do, but be sincere.

Most guys like smart women, but not smarter than them...
(If you are, don't make it known to them.)

Some guys tell you what you "want to hear" so they
can get what they want...
GIRLS, don't have "sex" to get love.
Sex is not a bargaining chip.

"One-nighters" or one night stands are
one time sex without emotional commitment.
"Casual sex" can be regular sex with friends.
This is also known as "friends with benefits". It's no "strings attached" sex.
There is no romantic involvement or a future of a committed relationship.

Do you really want that?

People's actions speak louder than words.
The two are sometimes not in sync.
This is why you need to pay attention to
not only their words but actions.

A guy should treat you like a lady.
It doesn't mean he should throw his jacket over a puddle for you to walk
over. He should, however, open a door and do other gentlemanly things for
you. It really comes down to showing respect and having good manners.
Remember always to thank him when he does.

There is a difference between flirting and being friendly with others.
Your intentions and desired outcome will define which of the two you and
others are doing.

Reserve your kisses for the person who you are in a relationship with.
Kiss the person you care about on the cheek, not the lips.

There are two types of jealousy: unhealthy and healthy.

People who display unwarranted jealousy in a relationship may be insecure, have fear of abandonment or want to control. Some repeated behaviors of unhealthy jealousy can be: constantly and obsessively checking up on you by calling several times a day to ask where you are, spying when you are out with your friends, looking at your phones text messages daily or questioning why you are a few minutes late coming home. He/she may even demand you don't spend time with your other friends.

Healthy jealousy, on the other hand, is normal when there is a real threat or uncertainty to your relationship. You need to address any feelings of jealousy or insecurities in your relationship right away.

Family comes before your friends, unless your friends are your family.

If you want good friends, you have to be a good friend.

Keep a few good friends no matter what the distance.

A good friend wants you to be happy and is happy for you.

Please don't let your friends drive drunk; give them a ride.

When you are not with your significant other, don't do anything (i.e. flirt)
you would not do in front of him.

Try to get help if you're in an abusive relationship.
Abuse can be physical or emotional.
Tell someone about it.
Don't keep it a secret.

Relationships are like an investment: if you are not getting enough interest,
move on...

Your first break up is hard.
Well, all break ups are hard but you will get through it.
Most think that their first love is their only love and they could never
possibly love again. Have faith, there is someone out there for you, and you
will love again. Use the time alone to become comfortable with who you are
and what you want before you start a relationship again.

Don't think you can change someone because you can't.
You can only change yourself.

CHAPTER 9

Love

Relationships

Love

Finances

Become good friends with the person before you start a romantic
relationship, and love should follow.

A girl should be subtle about showing that she is attracted to a guy. This
usually doesn't apply to guys. They tend to be more direct/ aggressive.
Why? Because they like a challenge- it's that primal instinct thing.

You can't force love.
Someone can hide behind the word "love "to fool you
but, when they show you love,
you can see the words in action.

Something good is always worth waiting for and the longer you wait
the better it could be.

Some guys may not say the words "I love you"
until they test the waters by saying things like:

We really have a deep connection.

Could you be with someone like me?

I think I'm starting to have feelings for you.

My mother would really like you.

You need to trust your "inner voice" that he's being sincere.

An experienced "player" knows how to play the game
to win you over for his own "sexual agenda".

If he asks you to meet his parents and/or family,
it's usually looking pretty safe.

Love is something you feel and it's hard to explain.
Sometimes it may feel as if you can't imagine your life without the
other person, or your heart skips a beat in anticipation to see them
again.

When that time comes, try to let the guy tell you he loves you first.
Remember, however, that some guys may need a "nudge" before he
tells you that.

Generally, it takes men longer to realize that they do.
If you can't wait, he may feel pressured to tell you "I love you".

Love is unlike, sex, love is a **process**.

So, give them that chance.

If all else fails, remember: whatever comes from the heart
is something you should never regret.

Love and sex are not the same…

Love and lust are not the same…

Having sex should be an intimate, deep and emotional connection that needs to be between two consenting adults.

"Hook-ups" are just a physical act of sex.

A lasting, and loving relationship will probably not start out as a "hook-up."

Know that boys do like flirtatious girls that "put out", but they typically want to marry a girl who doesn't get around.

Please don't be afraid to love.
You might regret the chance you did not take...

Try not to over use the words "I love you".

Some guys after saying "I love you" the first time, don't say it often again.
They think because they told you once you should know that they do;
you don't need to hear it again. Not to worry. They are just wired that way.

You need to give love to receive love.

When you find your soul mate, be careful that you don't become
roommates, and end up as cell mates.

The "In Love Feeling" is short lived. People are on their good behavior at first. They eventually will go back to who they really are. Then, the real work/joy of love starts. You need to remember and do the things that made you fall in love with each other initially and keep doing those things. If you don't keep doing them you can easily "fall out of love."

When you love someone you should try not to hurt their feelings.

Where there is love, there is unspoken trust.

"There can be no true love without trust."
~Elias A. Lianos

Don't be afraid to end a bad relationship because some need to end.

Love is doing something thoughtful and unexpected for the person you love.

When you love someone, you put their needs before yours.

When you are loved, you are high on your lover's priority list.

Love is giving him the last piece of chocolate cake: you've been saving for yourself.

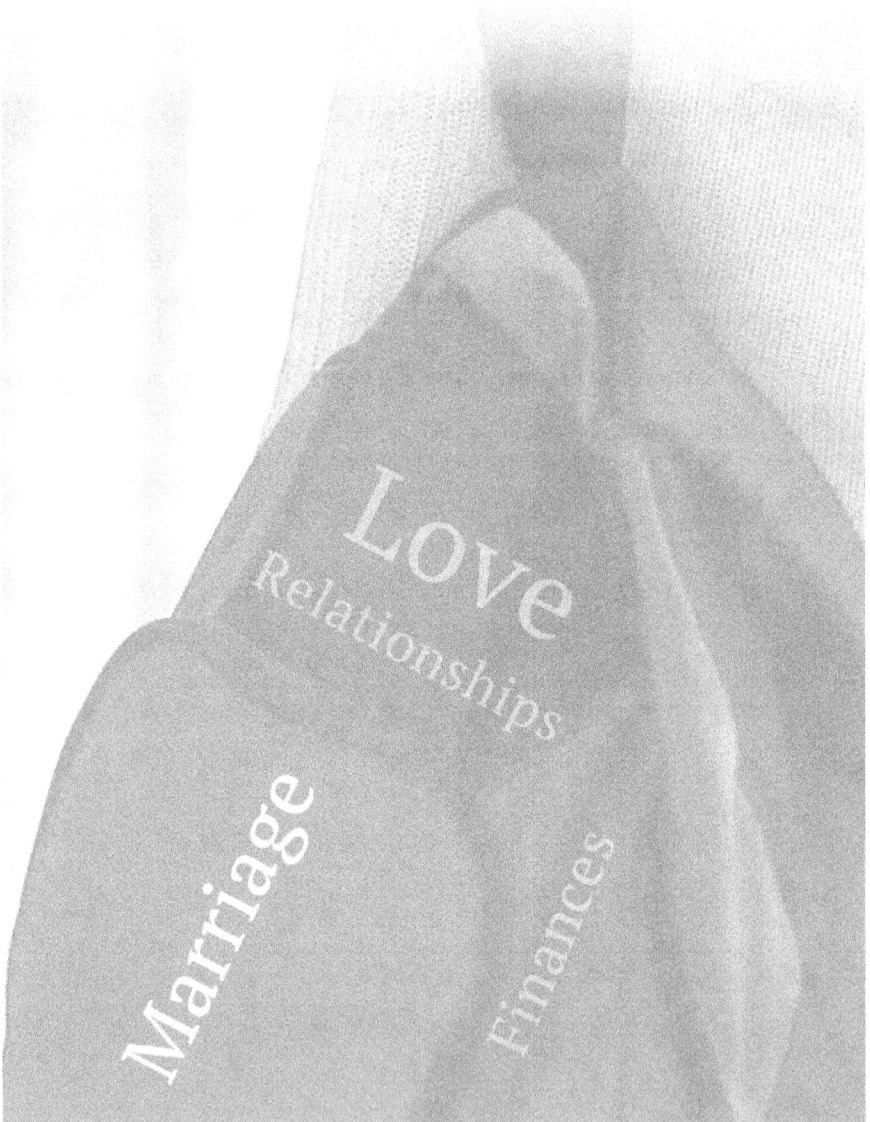

CHAPTER 10

Love

Relationships

Marriage

Finances

Marriage is a partnership.
Think of it like this: One person is behind the steering wheel of a car,
and the other person navigates.
Ideally, you take turns driving and navigating,
but don't go over the speed limit,
and try not to get lost.

Marriage is a commitment.
Don't feel that you have to get married because all your friends are getting
married. Do it for the right reasons. Ask yourself why you want to get
married and why not stay single?

If your intention is to marry your boyfriend, and you're not engaged don't
"live together" before marriage.
If you do he may lose the incentive to marry you.
(Why buy the DVD if you can keep watching it on Netflix?)

What do you think?

Try not to get caught up in the hype of a big, extravagant, and expensive wedding. Have a budget you can afford. Don't go into debt to fund your wedding. Your wedding day should not be viewed as a goal. Instead, the beginning of a new life with on-going goals to share with the person you love.

In a marriage, you need to work as team and be in alignment.

You can be a strong and successful career woman AND also be taken care of by a guy, but don't let it define you. What's even better: you can take care of each other.

Communication in a marriage is critical and so is laughter.

"Marriage is like a roller coaster... enjoy the ride"
~ Leo Melissourgos

Marriage is not all heavenly rainbows. It takes two people who make the decision to share one umbrella and survive the rain storm together. Have a big beautiful umbrella on hand...

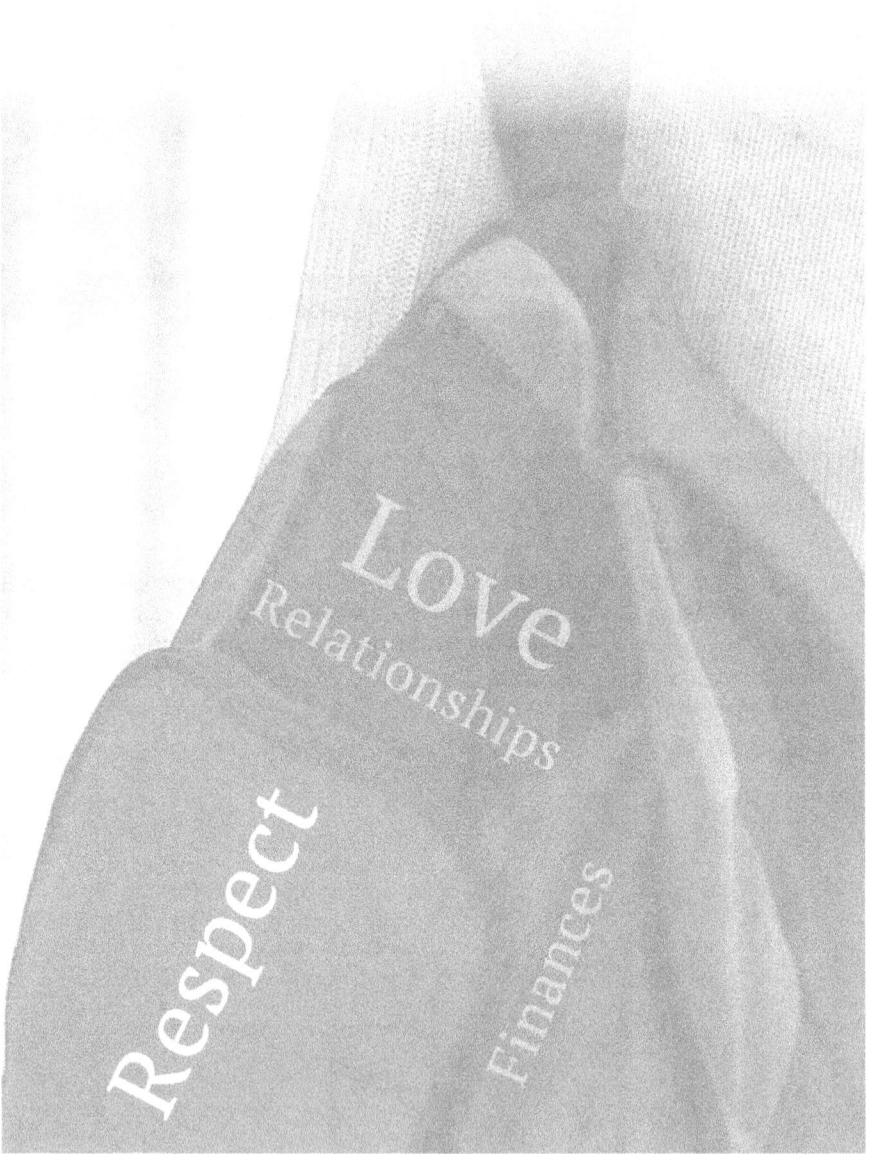

CHAPTER 11

Love

Relationships

Respect

Finances

It's a sign of respect to knock on a closed door.
(Also, be prepared for what you might see or find on the other side if you don't knock).

Call whenever you are going to be more than five minutes late for an appointment or date.

Respect yourself and others will too.

Be willing to show love and care toward other people, even strangers.

"Find the best way to remember the names of the people you meet; especially while you're still talking to them."
~Daniel V. Gonzalez

Never break a promise. Otherwise, don't make one.
Promises are presents in advance.
"Pinky promises" also count.

Return voicemails, emails, and text messages. :-D

Show respect to everyone. It doesn't matter what job they have
or what type of work they do.

"Respect and love go hand and hand."
~Christos Voulikis

Remember to always say "excuse me", "please", "thank you", and "you're welcome" too.

Sometimes people need a few seconds or hours to be alone with their thoughts. Respect the time they need or have requested from you.

Show respect for other people's feelings. Their feelings may not be the same as yours, but it doesn't mean that their feelings are not important or shouldn't be respected.

If you don't agree with someone else's opinion, it doesn't give you the right to disrespect him/her. You can agree to disagree.

Always wait your turn and don't skip.

If you are able to, offer your seat to the elderly or a pregnant woman. This applies anywhere: a restaurant, an airport, or train station.

Don't interrupt others when they are talking, unless you ask their permission.

Always make eye contact when speaking to someone. If you are uncomfortable, looking at the bridge of their nose when speaking to them makes it easier.

The tone and volume you use to communicate expresses the respect you have for the person.

Telling the truth is a sign of respect.

Being respectful towards others shows you have good manners.

Having self-respect will take you places you'll want to go.
Having no self-respect may take you places you shouldn't go.

Respect should be non-negotiable.

Remember to pick up after yourself; the maid is on vacation.

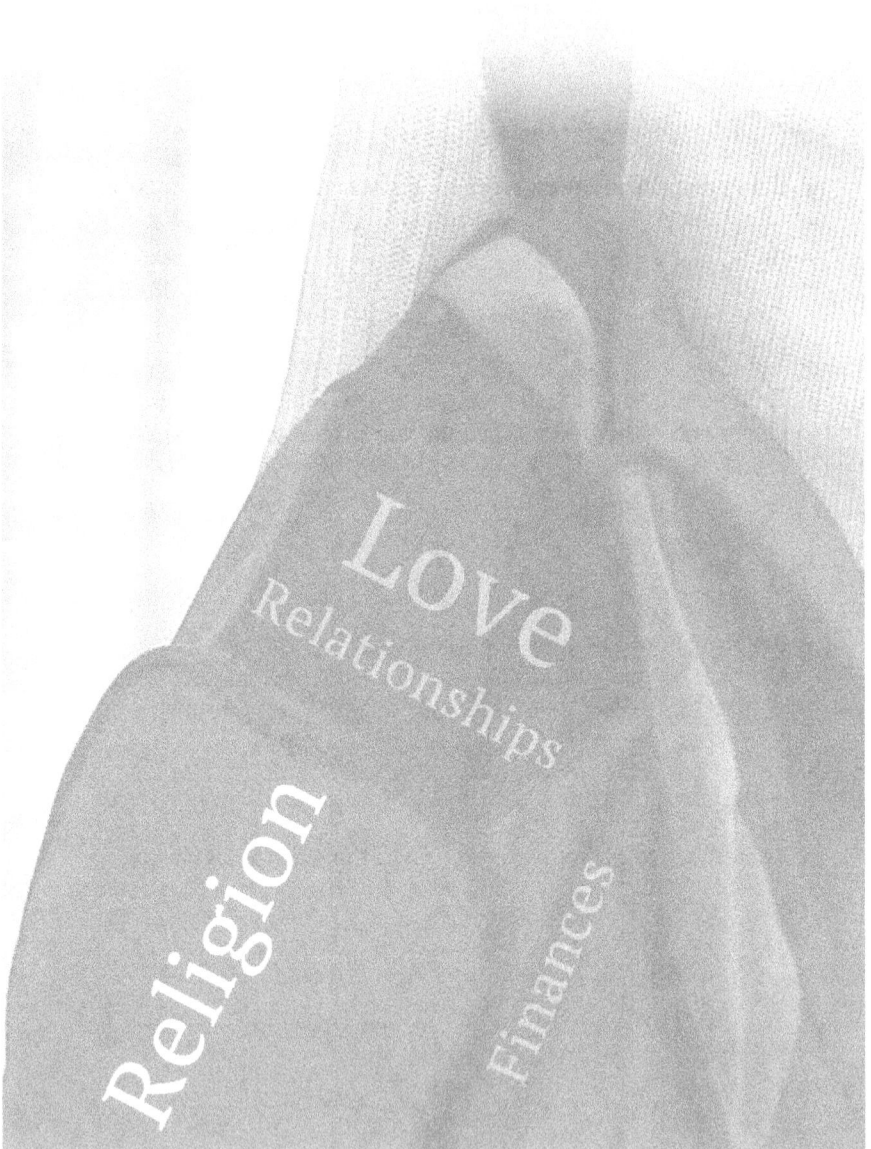

CHAPTER 12

Love
Relationships
Religion
Finances

Respect other people's religion even if you don't agree with it.

"Don't pray for things. Pray for wisdom, courage, and guidance."
~Frank Gonzalez-1972

God sometimes speaks through the actions and voice of others.
(Psst...pay attention)

We meet people in our lives for a reason.
Some people may feel like God has sent them.
Free will lets you decide if you want them to stay or if you let them go.

Love Is patient, love is kind and is not jealous; love does not brag and is not arrogant, does not act unbecomingly; it does not seek its own, is not provoked, does not take into account a wrong suffered, does not rejoice in unrighteousness, but rejoices with the truth; bears all things, believes all things, hopes all things, endures all things.
1 Corinthians 13- New American Standard Bible (NASB).

Treat people the way you would like to be treated.

"Put your sword back into its place; for all who take up the sword
shall perish by the sword"
Matthew 26:52- New American Standard Bible (NASB).
(Those who use violence will be a victim of violence)

"God helps those who help themselves."
(Aesop, Greek Story Teller)

"Talk less and pray more..."
~Bob Gountis

It's best to always forgive. Know that forgiving is not saying its ok...
Sometimes you just got to let it go.

Always love your brother and your sister too.

The recommendation and belief has always been to wait
until marriage to have sex.
If you decide not to wait until marriage, know that the person you have sex
with will share a soul tie with you.
Two bodies become one, and you will carry that soul tie forever.

"Faith is like Wi-Fi:
It's invisible, but it has the power to connect you to what you need."
(Unknown Author)

Prayer can be powerful.

The Holy Bible is the best-selling book of all time,
sold and gifted world-wide.

It's been noted and believed by many that the Holy Bible is the most stolen
book. This can make you wonder, why it's the most stolen book?

(It's also ironic because "thou shalt not steal" is one of the Ten
Commandments.)

Believing in something is better than believing in nothing.

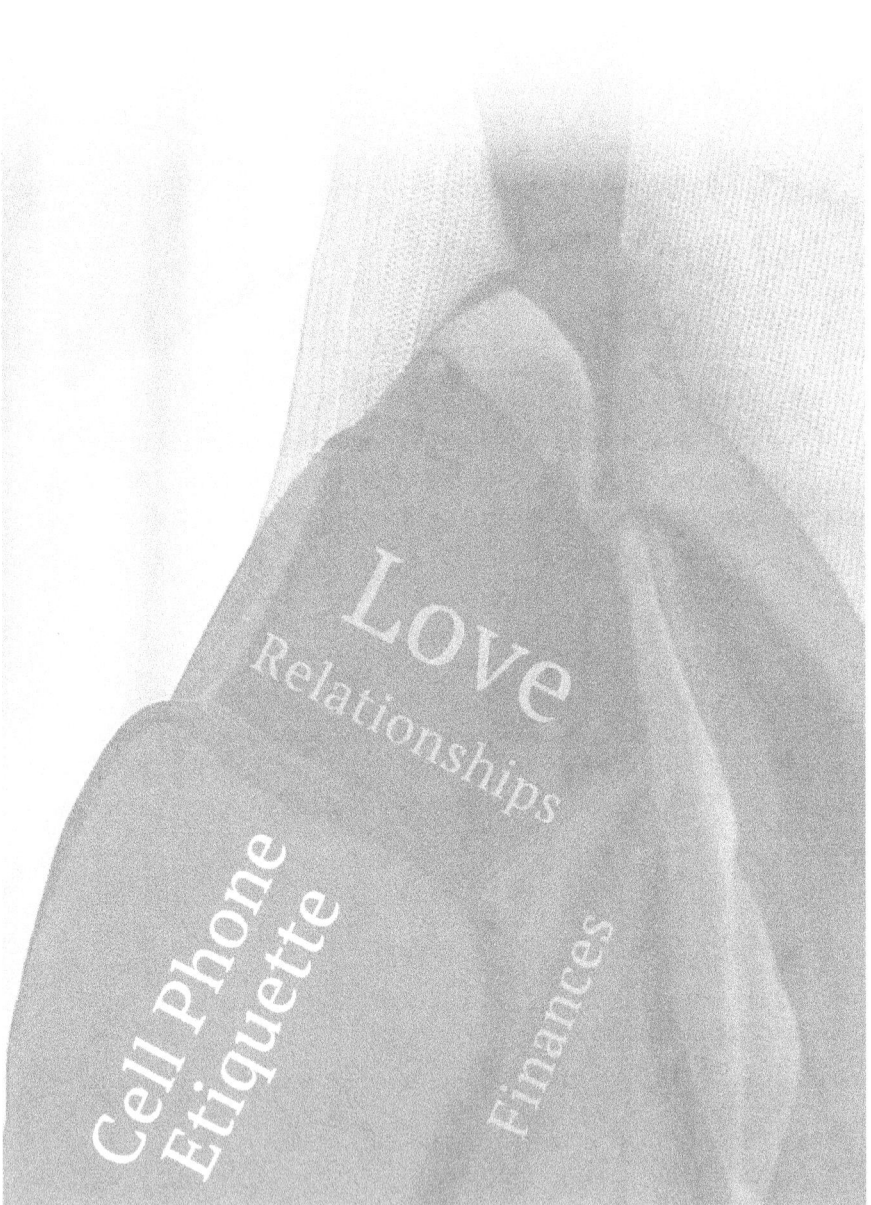

Chapter 13

Love

Relationships

Cell Phone
Etiquette

Finances

While having dinner with others, try not to use your cell phone.

Focus on the person you are with, not your phone.

When in a meeting or an appointment, put your phone on vibrate or silent.

Remember not to use your phone in a public bathroom.
You never know who might be in the stall next to you.

Ask permission to view photos on someone's cell phone.
If he/she is only showing you one photo, it is not polite to scroll through
the rest or take over their phone.

Have a professional sounding ring tone or have your phone on vibrate
when at work. Follow the company's cell phone policies regarding when
you can use your phone. (Instead of talking on the phone, text if you can;
it's less distracting to others around you).

Remember to turn your cell phone on silent while watching a movie at the theater; it is very distracting to others around you if you don't and the phone goes off.

A good rule of thumb: if your call is disconnected, whoever initiated the call should call back first.

Remember that you or others may not understand the intent of a text because the tone of the words and body language are missing.

Please don't break up with someone over text.

If you are expecting an important call, let the person you are with know that, when the time comes, excuse yourself to take the call.

Have an important conversation in person,
not through a text or over the phone.

> *I can't he-a-r
> you... We're
> b-r-e-a-king
> up....*

> *Huh, what...I...
> didn't know we
> were dating?*

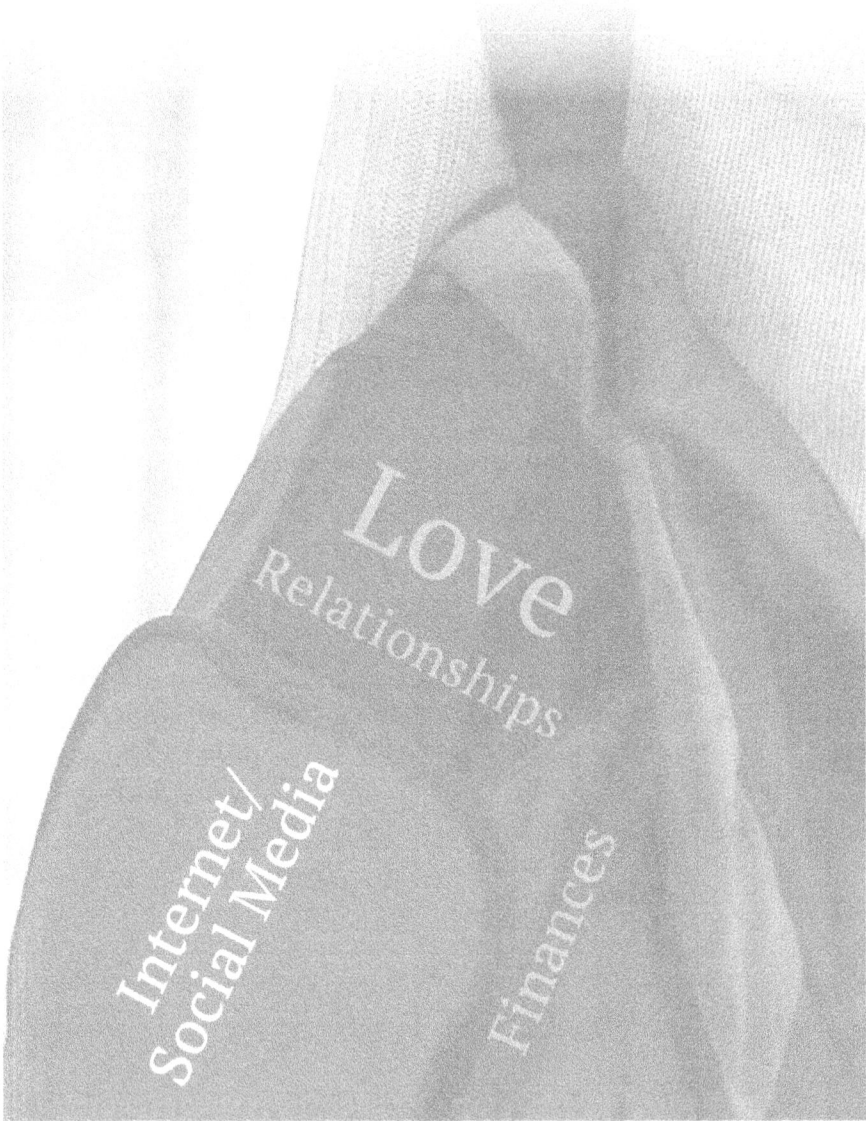

CHAPTER 14

Love

Relationships

Internet/
Social Media

Finances

You shouldn't believe or trust everything you read on the Internet!

Remember that social media is public. Don't display yourself on Facebook, Twitter, Vine, Instagram or any of the other media out there if you don't want your boss, significant other, mother, father or the rest of the world to know your business. Social media is building a dossier on you!

Snapchats are deleted automatically, but they are also stored in the cloud. There is no guarantee that they are deleted within a certain time frame. In addition, this doesn't prevent someone taking a screen shot and saving or sharing the photo. Technology can be complicated and is constantly changing so you need to be aware of all this, the next time you snap.

I know it sounds CREEPY... but potential employers do look you up on social media to find out what kind of person you are.
It's easy to do: "google" your name and see what comes up.
Surprising, isn't it...?

Have you wondered what the cloud is? "The cloud" is a metaphor for "the internet". Something that is stored in the cloud means the information is located and accessed from a network of servers, instead of your computer's hard drive or cell phone. It's like a storage center. For example, when you store your photos on Dropbox or Google Drive you are storing them in the cloud.

When using social media represent yourself in the best light; otherwise it could embarrass you months or years later.

Remember: when you write emails, they are not private; they're stored in the cloud and can be printed.

Use a secure WIFI connection when possible because
it protects your information from being stolen.
The additional benefit of using Wi-Fi is that it saves on your data charges.

Re-read your emails, posts and tweets before you HIT the send button. (This is especially important if you are upset).

Remember not to share too much by tweeting every detail of your life.

If you are sending an email remember to add a subject in the subject line.

It's true; spell check doesn't always give you the correct spelling of a word. The auto correct feature on your cell phone can give you some pretty funny substitutions so re-read before sending.

Selfies can be a great expression and are fun to share. Don't overdo it.
There have been accidents reported while taking selfies.
Believe it or not, some people have inadvertently caused a car crash or even fallen off a cliff while taking selfies.

Keep your passwords safe, and DO NOT share them with anyone.
Try not use the same password for everything.
Change your passwords often.
I know it's a time consuming pain...

Don't enter personal data like your credit card or your social security
numbers if the website is not secure. It will have an "S" for secure in the
web address. (i.e. http**s**)

Protect your phone and other electronic devices,
and be careful of web surfers looking over your shoulder.
Note: They don't always wear Hawaiian surfing shirts.

Be aware of "phishing". Phishing is a way of luring and the attempt to steal your personal information like user names, passwords and credit card information. Phishers are clever and masquerade as people from reputable and legitimate companies. They will do it over email, phone, or through social media.

Be aware of "spear phishing" attacks. They are emails that you receive from a "friend or business" that looks like it's really from them. They (hackers) know your name and use it in the email addressed to you. They can get your information from recent on-line purchases or from posts you made on social networking sites. Hackers will attempt to get your passwords. They also ask in the email for you to take action immediately or to open a document they have sent.

If you get suspicious emails or voice messages, report it.

All this means keep up with technology.

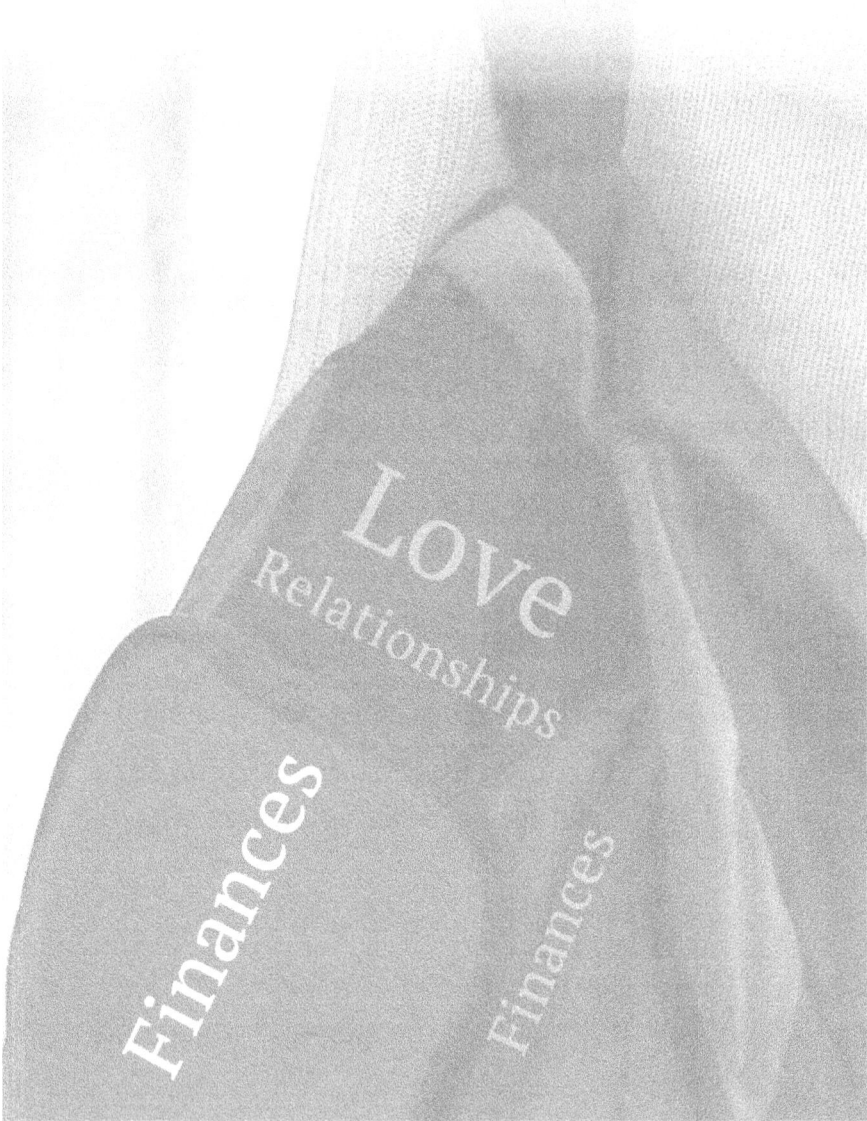

CHAPTER 15

When you turn 18 years old (WHOO HOO!), you become a legal adult. Don't sign your name on any contracts or documents without reading and understanding them. Don't be afraid to ask questions.

Your credit score starts at age 18. A credit score is a report card of how you manage your money. If you have a good report card, you are loaned money, and if you don't have a good report card, you might not be able to get a loan. It's calculated based on the history of how you pay your bills. If you pay them on time it helps your credit score positively. Also, paying on time avoids interest which is extra money you pay to the lender. You might not think this is important right now, but your credit history follows you for a long time. Your credit report is reviewed when renting an apartment, leasing or financing a car. Some employers, depending on the job you are interviewing for, will look at your credit score as a measure of your character and dependability.

You are responsible to pay your own debts or fulfill any agreements you have signed.
(Not your parents).

If you have "CC's" (credit cards), use them only for convenience.
All you really only need is one credit card, maybe two at most.
Try to pay the balance off every month.

Once you get out of school, have at least $200.00-$300.00 stashed at
home you never know if you will need it case of an emergency.
Hopefully you will never need it.

Try to save at least 10% of each paycheck in the bank or some type of an
investment.

You can learn to budget your money. Create a system, it could be an excel spreadsheet or even a note book. Write down how much money you have coming in and how much you have going out through bills and expenses. This provides a basis on how you spend your money and it helps you create a budget.

Save at least a 3 to 4 month salary once you start working as a backup. This is in case you have to change jobs or something unexpected happens and you need money to pay your bills.

When the time comes and you want to buy a house or condo, try to get a 15 -20 year mortgage. The shorter the term of the mortgage, the less amount of interest you pay. You will need a down payment which may be 10%-20% of the sales price. Interest is extra money you pay the bank or lender for the money that was loaned to you.
Why should the banks charge interest?

Keep a constant eye on the interest rates. You may want to re-finance your loan to avoid paying interest on the money that you borrowed. You can use that extra money to put towards your loan to pay it off in the same amount of time or less. If you are not good with numbers or finances ask someone who is.

"Bean by bean the sack gets filled"
(Saving a little bit at a time adds up)
(Greek Proverb)

If you're trying to save money look at the little things that you buy. Drinking coffee, latte's or other drinks daily at $4.00 a day adds ups. Let's do some simple math: $4.00 x 7 days a week = $28.00.
$28.00 x 4 weeks a month = $112.00
$112.00 x 12 months = $1.344.00 a year.

What could you do with that extra money?

When you want to buy something, ask yourself, do you really need it or do you just want it? Can you really afford it?

Remember to try and control your money, but don't let it control you.

Whoever pays the bills makes the rules.
Let your children know that if and when you have them.

Never count on someone else's money; make your own.

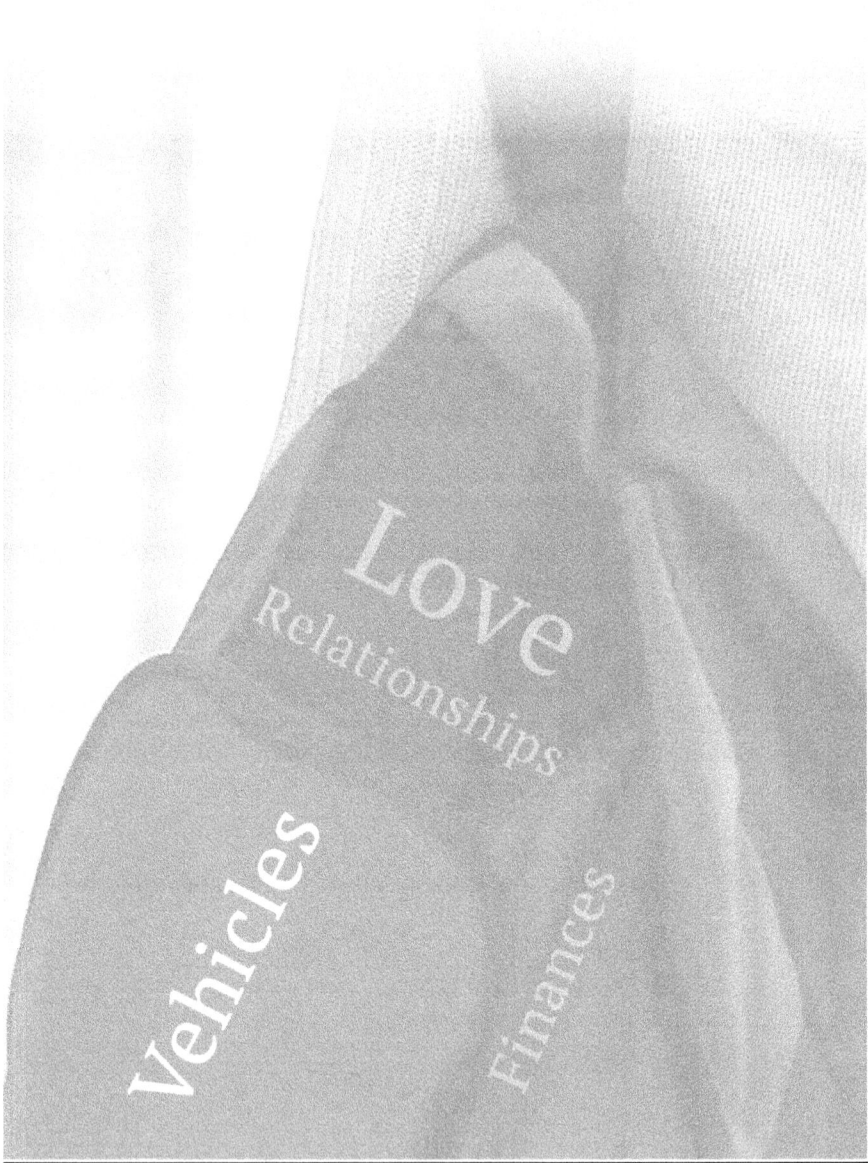

CHAPTER 16

Love

Relationships

Vehicles

Finances

"Have your parents review the rules of driving
before teaching you to drive."
~Amalia Melissourgos

Your car is one of the most expensive and important possessions you will
own.
Take care of it.

Change the oil on your car at least every 3,000- 5,000 miles.
Also, learn how to check the fluid levels.

Buy new tires when you need them.

If your brakes start feeling or sounding funny,
don't wait to have them checked out.

Keep your registration and insurance card in the glove box.

111

If you get the opportunity to learn to drive a car with a stick shift, do it. It's fun and you never know when you may need to drive one.

Be an attentive driver.

Always wear your seat belt and request that your passengers do to.

Talking on the phone while driving is distracting, it doesn't matter if you are using hands-free or the speaker. You need to be focused on driving. In some states, you can be pulled over and ticketed for talking on your cell phone if you are not using a hands-free device. The best advice: don't talk on the phone while driving in any state.

When you borrow someone's vehicle, return it clean with a full gas tank.

PLEASE   DON'T   TEXT   AND   DRIVE!

Oh by the way...

PLEASE   DON'T   TEXT   AND   DRIVE!

Did I mention...

PLEASE   DON'T   TEXT   AND   DRIVE!

Have I said...

PLEASE   DON'T   TEXT   AND   DRIVE!

HAVE YOU FILLED HER BACKPACK?

If you ever get pulled over by the police, stay cool. Roll down your window; keep both hands on the steering wheel until you are asked for your driver's license. Don't get out of your vehicle, unless you are asked to.
Be respectful and address the officer as sir.
You need to be honest and cooperative when asked,
"why do you think you were pulled over?"

If an unmarked squad car pulls you over and the officer asks you to get out of the vehicle, ask to see his/her identification. If your gut is telling you something doesn't seem right or you feel that you are in danger, call 911 to verify. The dispatcher will know if there is an unmarked squad in your area.

If you are in a rear end collision call 911 immediately and then your parents.

Get a second opinion or estimate on any car repairs.

Remember: park 15 feet away from a fire hydrant.

Always negotiate the price when buying a new or used car. You need to know that the auto industry is predominately male. The assumption is that girls don't know much about cars. You may feel more comfortable taking your boyfriend, brother, uncle or father along the first time, but only if they can help.
Note: You may also have a pretty cool aunt who knows how to negotiate a deal, and you might want to take her.

When buying a car, beware of the question.
How much are you willing to spend?
"They will try to sell the least amount of car for that amount of money."
~Daniel V. Gonzalez

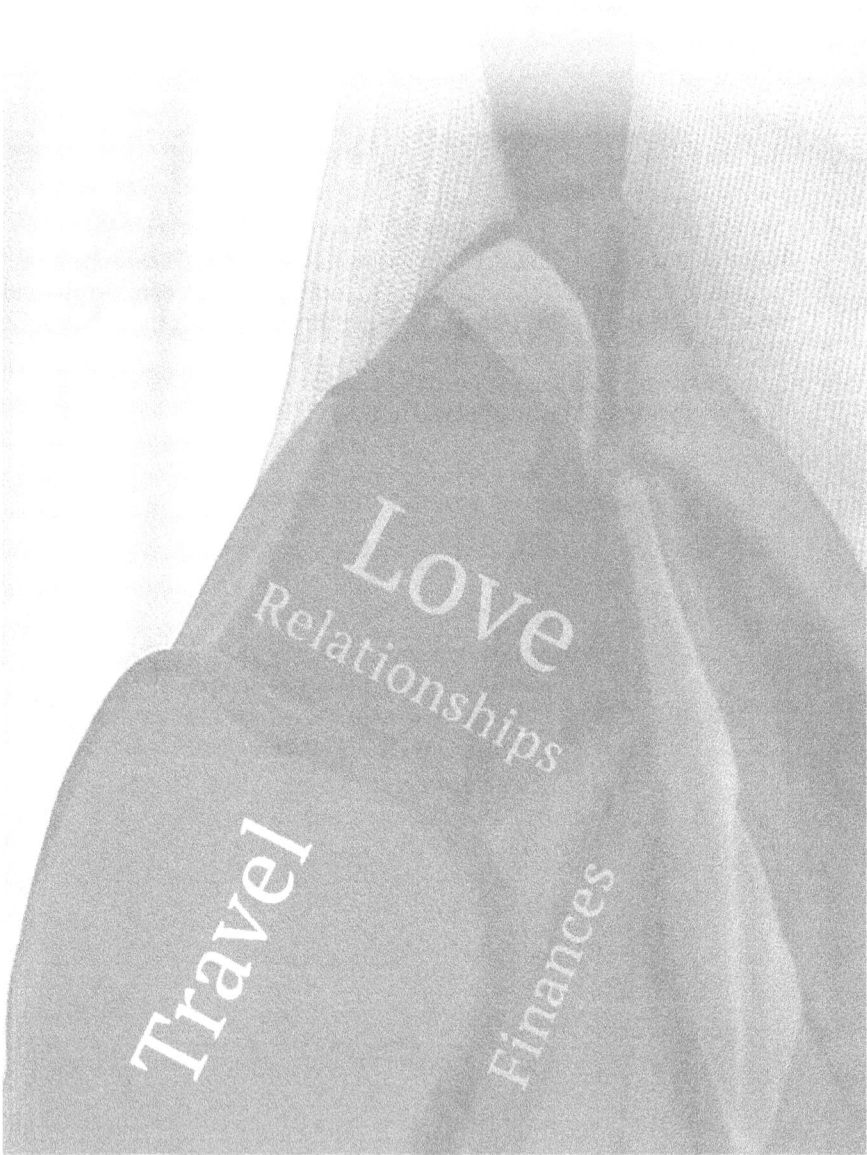

CHAPTER 17

If you have the opportunity travel and see the world.

Do some research on the location you plan to travel to.

Make a check list of items that you will need for the trip.

Don't over pack because you never end up wearing everything.

Have a change of under clothes, shirt, tooth brush and tooth paste in your carry on. Plane delays and lost luggage do happen, and it's nice to have those things on hand if it does.

Remember to pack that good pair of walking shoes.

"If traveling to a foreign country, learn about their culture, and some of their basic words for communication."
~Amalia Melissourgos

Check to see if you need a passport. If you already have one, make sure you re-new it several months before your travel dates.

Do you need immunizations prior to going to that country?

Check to see if you need an international driver's license, in case you would like to rent a car and drive in that country.

Contact your wireless provider and ask questions about the cellular service in the area that you are traveling.

Ask your wireless provider if you need to turn on or add a data package.

Will you incur roaming charges, if so what are the rates?

Does the hotel offer free Wi-Fi?

Before you leave for your vacation or trip, make your bed with clean sheets. It is nice to come home to your own bed with fresh sheets.

Leave your home tidy with dishes and glasses put away. Also, unplug small appliances like a toaster or coffee pot.

Keep your valuables on you or in your purse or backpack when in transit.

Never leave your things unattended!

"Travel in pairs/groups."
~Amalia Melissourgos

When on vacation don't take off on your friends or leave them behind
for something that may seem better.

If you take a taxi cab, know that some taxi cab drivers may take advantage
of tourists by driving them around in circles to charge higher fares.

"If you're are converting or exchanging currency (money),
look at the fluctuating rates.
Each bank provides different rates and it varies day to day."
~Konstantinos Kokalis

Learn the exchange rate of the foreign currency especially when paying for
things. Sometimes tourists are taken advantage of by the owners of
restaurants or shops. Review the bill and the money you receive back from
your transaction. Also, remember to ask for a receipt.

Learn military time (24 hour clock) and how to convert it. An easy way to do so is by subtracting 12 from the 24 hour time.
Example: 17:00 hrs-12:00 hrs. = 5:00 p.m.

Take a lot of photos.

"Make a photo album of your trip.
They are cool to look at and reminisce about."
~Amalia Melissourgos

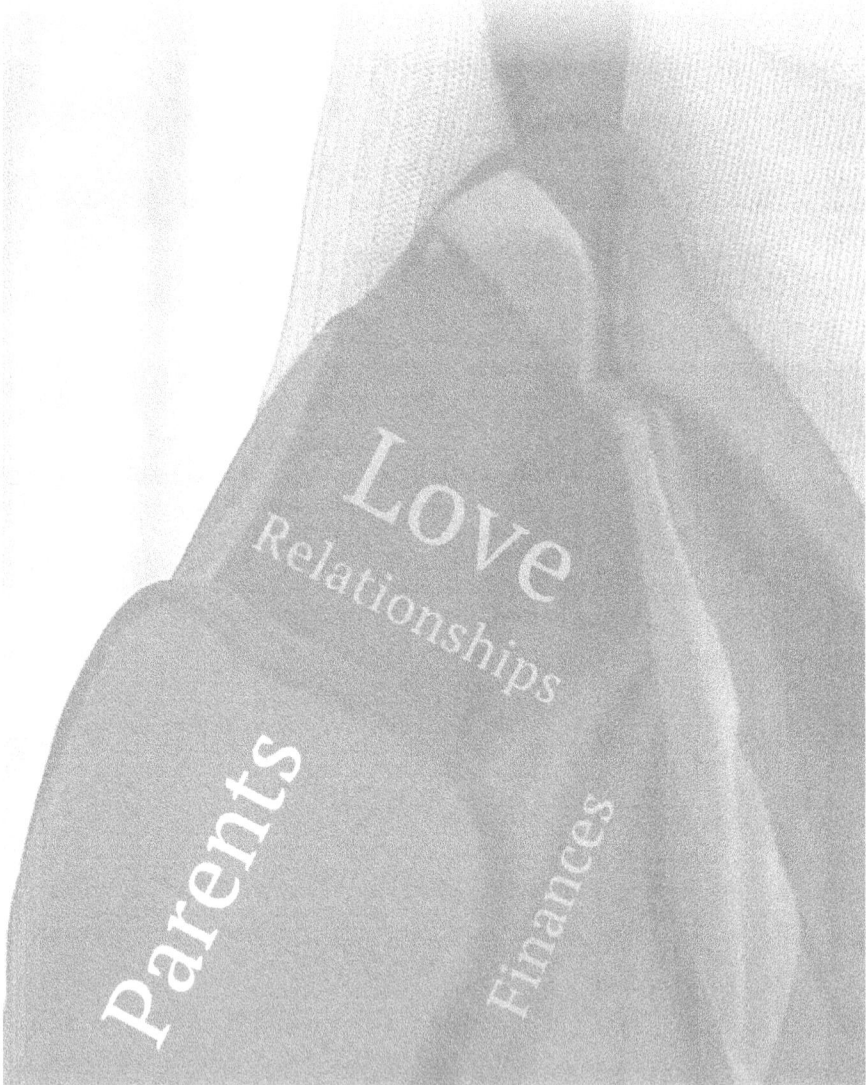

CHAPTER 18

Love

Relationships

Parents

Finances

Not everyone lives in a two parent home. It sometimes doesn't work out that way. Know that it's okay. You need to accept whatever situation you or your friends are in, and make the best of it.

Sometimes we don't understand why our parents do what they do...
until later in life.

You are responsible for your own actions. You can't blame a bad situation entirely on your upbringing because you make the choice to be who you are and do what you do.

Parents and caregivers are teachers.

Remember that parents were once teenagers.
Shh...that's why they sometimes have insight on things.

Parents can make mistakes too; not all of them are *aliens*...

If you become a parent, it is one the most important responsibilities you
will ever have, and a life changing one too. Fasten your seat belt.

Please try to get to know your parents before it's too late!

There are role models all around you. Determine who the good ones are. You can also learn what not to do from the less desirable ones.

When your parent's age, which is inevitable, there are responsibilities that need to be taken care of. When you become older, you may need to have those tough conversations with them.

I still can't figure out where parents have hidden those eyes on the back of their head!

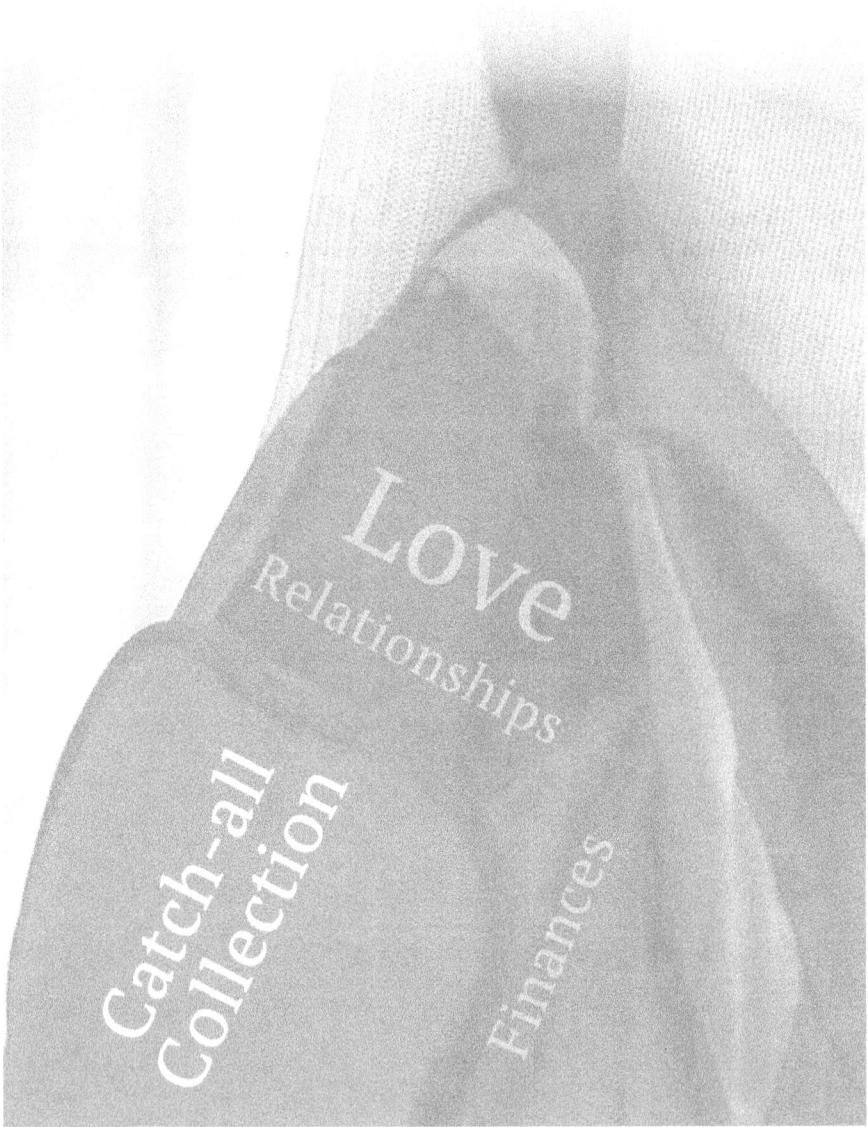

CHAPTER 19

Love

Relationships

Catch-all
Collection

Finances

"If you are depressed, you are living in the past. If you are anxious, you are living in the future. If you are at peace, you are living in the present."
-Lao Tzu

Sometimes you just have to live life one day at a time, to get over or work through whatever is troubling you.

Try to live your life without regrets. There will come a time you will reflect back on your life and you might regret the things you didn't do.

Always do more than what is expected.

If you want to meet an interesting person, maybe you need to be an interesting person.

People can basically fall into three categories: The maestros in life, the observers in life, and the ones who wake up one morning and ask themselves what the heck has happen to my life.
What category do you want to be in?

Have lots of pretty shoes!
Note: At least 25 pairs if not more.

Adults go through stages in life; sometimes they last decades. They want a big beautiful house and then they want to down size later in life.
Perhaps there is something to be said about adopting some of the minimalist attitude early in life. Having a lot of material possessions can be meaningless. Find what gives your life meaning and purpose, but still keep the pretty shoes too.

"There is no right way to do the wrong thing."
(Unknown Author)

Treat yourself to fresh flowers,
and put them in a beautiful vase.

Be Confident; it's always an attractive quality to have.
Know however, there is a difference in having confidence and being
arrogant.

Live in the moment, but be responsible.

Never think that apologizing is a weakness.
It is strength to admit you are wrong.

International fun superstition: If you give a purse or wallet as a gift, always include a small amount of money inside. If you do, the person's wallet or purse will always be filled with money.

Remember: when using a screwdriver; righty tighty, lefty loosey.

Have dreams and make them big!

Find what you are passionate about and do it!

Explore and try new things

Sing in the shower!
It's also okay if you feel as if you have to cry in there too.
(Perfect place so one can hear you).

"Learn Spanish."
~Leo Melissourgos

Sometimes in life you need to use the KISS principal:
"Keep it Simple Stupid" – (noted by the US Navy in 1960)
Or "Keep it short and simple."

Don't judge a book by its cover; you don't know the "inside" story.

"When you hear of many cherries, bring a small basket."
(Greek Proverb)

Have a robust vocabulary.

Learn to tell good stories!
Story telling has been around for centuries.

Try to avoid the four "hot" topics that can cause arguments:
sex, politics, money and religion.

If you find what you are passionate about, the hours will feel like minutes.

Always have a back-up plan when there is high stakes involved, and when
in doubt.

Harboring anger and resentment towards people is allowing them to live rent-free in your mind. Let them go, kick them out, or start charging them rent.

"Insanity:
doing the same thing over and over again and expecting different results."
~Albert Einstein

Try camping once in your life; breathe in the fresh air; close your eyes and enjoy the silence if only for a moment.

Learn to cook delicious food.

Have a cool signature.

Don't live in clutter.

Be organized with your thoughts and possessions.

You learn a lot from the drunk, the young, and the old because they have little or no filters which mean they speak the truth.

Have someone take you fishing once in your life. Fishing brings serenity and your stress dissipates. The exception when the fish start to bite.

Adopt these 4 rules of Fishing:

1. Have someone else bait your hook.
2. Have someone else take the fish off the hook.
3. Have someone else clean your fish.
4. Learn and be able to tell your own fisherman tales.

Everything happens for a reason, but we might not know the reason
or lesson until much later.

Make a bucket list of things you want to do, see, learn,
achieve and accomplish.
Start it now.

The familiar road is the one you have taken before and it may be shorter.
The road never taken may be a longer one, but it's the one we learn the
most from.

Learn to sew a button back on your clothing.
If you can, sew it back on right away so you don't lose the button.

135

Plant a garden at least once in your life.

When you cook meals, remember to add
the secret ingredient of love.
Note: It might sound corny, but the food does really taste better.

Volunteer your time and give back.

Think before you ink.
A tat is permanent.

"When you get into the dance, remember to finish the dance."
(Greek Proverb)

Learn to appreciate what you have; even if you don't have much there are
others who may have less than you.

Keep a journal of your thoughts and dreams or anything worth
remembering. Try to be disciplined and write daily.
It could be funny or inspiring to read years later.
Note: You might also decide to burn it later in life
so your kids don't find and read it...

If you take the last cookie, don't leave an empty box in the cupboard.

"Even if you put your name on something to save for later,
someone else might still eat it."
~Amalia Melissourgos

The harder you work for something, the more you will appreciate it.

Life has so many twists and turns sometimes you need to be spontaneous.

Don't give others your garage code.
It's basically giving away the key to your house.

Learn to play golf. It's good exercise. But what's even better,
it will certainly impress the boys and they might even let you join the club...

If you have nothing good to say, don't say anything at all.

Find a productive way to manage your stress.
It could be reading, writing or exercising.

"Where you are, I have been, and where I am, you will be."
(Greek Proverb)

Some parents buy and fill your backpack.

Some parents only buy or only fill your backpack.

Sometimes parents don't know how to fill a backpack.

There is nothing wrong with any of this,

and during your lifetime you should keep filling it yourself.

If you have the chance, try filling someone else's too.

Notes

About the Author

Elizabeth Kokalis was born in America to Greek immigrants who left their country for the new world. Her parents were strict traditionalists who kept and enforced old values and mores. It's all they knew and felt comfortable in keeping. They tried to protect her by giving ridiculous curfews like requesting her to come home when the street lights came on. She couldn't even go out on dates. She was viewed as a good little Greek girl at home and an assertive American girl to the outside world. It was tricky for her a to find that balance. She felt split between two worlds.

Getting an education was her ticket to freedom; otherwise, she might have been forced into marriage. Her parents upon high school graduation gave her a choice to go to school or get married. She wanted to be a rebel and not entertain any type of pre-arranged marriage. She needed to pave her own way and start a new journey of her own.

Elizabeth earned a B.S. in Social Welfare from the University of Wisconsin-Milwaukee. She worked as a social worker after graduating and also volunteered her time in several non-profit organizations. After a short time in the field, she pursued a career in sales. Elizabeth works in the wireless communications industry as a successful business sales professional and has been with the same company for over 25 years. Her experience included serving in both management and non-management roles during her career.

www.ingramcontent.com/pod-product-compliance
Lightning Source LLC
LaVergne TN
LVHW021346080426
835508LV00020B/2134